101
a Tra
Needs to Know

101 Things a Translator Needs to Know

"I wish I could make this required reading for any freelancer wanting to pitch us ... brimming with good advice – from oft-forgotten 'basics' to several very subtle points – it's brilliantly and engagingly written. Pitch-perfect!"

David Jemielity, Head of Translations,
Banque Cantonale Vaudoise, Switzerland

"It's full of wise words and useful tips ... I would recommend it to anyone starting out in the profession."
David Bellos, author of Is That a Fish in your Ear? *and Director of Princeton University's Program in Translation and Intercultural Communication*

"In 101 Things a Translator Needs to Know some of the wittiest, pithiest, most level heads in the industry explain it all: signs that you're charging too much or too little (in 127 words), the fundamental difference between interpreters and translators (89 words), how to create an ergonomic setup in your office (96 words). You've got time to read this."
Corinne McKay, freelance translator and author of How to Succeed as a Freelance Translator *and* Thoughts on Translation: the Book

101 Things a Translator Needs to Know

WLF Think Tank

Compiled and edited by
Ian Hinchliffe, Terry Oliver, Ros Schwartz

Illustrated by Catherine A. Hiley

Published by WLF 101 Publishing 2014

Library of Congress Cataloging in Publication Data:
A catalogue record for this book has been requested.

ISBN: 978-91-637-5411-1

First edition published April 2014

For information, contact: info@101things4translators.com

This book is published by WLF 101 Publishing.

The authors are members of the WLF Think Tank, a virtual body of experienced practising translators. A full list of contributors appears at the end of the book.

Disclaimer: The publisher and the authors make no representations or warranties with respect to the accuracy or completeness of the contents of this work and specifically disclaim all warranties, including without limitation warranties of fitness for a particular purpose. The advice and strategies contained herein may not be suitable for every situation. This work is sold with the understanding that the publisher and authors are not professionally engaged in providing legal, financial, tax or career planning advice. If professional assistance is required, the services of a competent professional person should be sought. Neither the publisher nor the authors shall be liable for damages arising from the contents of this book. The fact that an organisation or website is referred to in this work as a citation and/or a potential source of further information does not mean that the author or the publisher endorses the information the organisation or website may provide or recommendations it may make. Readers should be aware that Internet websites listed in this work may have changed or disappeared between when this work was written and when it is read.

Project coordinators: Chris Durban, Ian Hinchliffe, Hugh Keith, Terry Oliver, Ros Schwartz

Book design: Mark Richardson

Introduction

This is a book for beginners. It's also a book for seasoned professionals, students and teachers. For freelancers and staff translators. For amateurs and experts, generalists and super-specialists – be they certified and sworn, recognised, authorised … or simply tantalised by translation's potential for a varied and enriching career.

101 Things a Translator Needs to Know is a compilation of insights from a broad spectrum of successful translation professionals with some 500 years of collective experience in fields ranging from highly technical to literary. No gripes, no grouses, just a selection of practical tips pointing in the direction of solutions.

Some of the headlines and topics send contradictory messages, you say? That's only natural: the translator's world is full of paradoxes, with no universal truths, not even for the simplest tasks. It all depends on the medium, the context and the end use.

And it's not just the wide range of document types and media. The industry itself is fragmented – and fragmenting further all the time. Most obviously, in terms of language pairs and directions, but also as a result of each individual practitioner's positioning on the generalist-specialist spectrum and in the time-quality-cost triangle. Some work as staff translators, others as freelancers supplying either agencies or direct clients; some edit high-volume computer-assisted translations while others specialise in finely crafted texts that are the product of in-depth subject knowledge and broad linguistic expertise.

There's fragmentation, too, among clients – between the users of translation services and those, often within the same organisation, who pay for them. For the former, the priority is quality; for the latter, more often than not, it is cost.

In this complex and competitive environment, it's up to translators to stake out their position, aware of their strengths and limitations, and aware, too, of the amount of research needed to complete a job satisfactorily. Most important of all, they need passion.

To close, a word to aspiring translators: like anything worth doing, translation is a hard profession to break into. But if you succeed, you can look forward to an intellectually stimulating working life with privileged insights into virtually all aspects of today's world. And make no mistake: as a freelance translator in particular, once you have acquired expert skills, solid experience, a portfolio of clients and a network of colleagues, you'll be well on your way to success. The authors of this book all love what they do and they hope their tips and advice will help you enjoy an equally fulfilling and rewarding lifestyle.

1

Translators don't translate words – they translate meaning

Machines and dictionaries translate words. But it takes a thinking, reasoning human being to translate what words mean.

Consider how you would translate the simple command "Shoot", depending on whether the person doing the shooting is a soldier, a footballer, a photographer, a gambler throwing dice, or a friend with something to tell you that you are eager to hear. The key here, as in all translation, is context.

2

A translation qualification is like a driving licence

Your degree or other language qualification marks the successful end of one process, but also the beginning of another. Like a driving licence, it means you can now move out into the world and start gaining experience. It doesn't mean your technique is flawless – the fact is, it never will be. But it does allow you to embark on the lifelong task of perfecting your skills.

Be aware that just as you can always be a better driver, you can always be a better translator.

3

Timing
it right

Looking for business? Prospective clients are busy people juggling 199 burning issues at any given time. On a normal day, translation won't rank much higher than 198th – or 200th.

So pick your moment to connect: even the busiest potential client is more likely to listen if their company is about to list on the stock market (all those foreign investors …) or take part in a major trade fair (all those foreign buyers …).

Track client events and identify windows of opportunity before you make your move. A timely pitch is far more likely to get you on their radar screen.

4

Don't get egg
on your face

Think twice before taking on a job in a specialist area that's outside your comfort zone. How much terminological support will you get from the client? Is this an area you can work your way into at short notice? How much time will it take? You might end up regretting taking on a job you can't complete to the required level of quality. In other words: learn to say no.

5

If you can't be
on time, be early

It's no good delivering a brilliant translation the day after the meeting for which it was needed. Delivering on time – despite the tribulations this may involve – is a cardinal rule. For your client, 90 per cent quality on time is usually preferable to 100 per cent an hour too late.

If the deadline is tight, make this clear before you accept the job. Explain the possible consequences, but do so in a positive way. Remind the client of the old adage, "the impossible we do at once; miracles take a little longer".

6

Always
reply

You know the scenario. You're busy, busy, busy working on that urgent translation. Who has time to answer the phone or read emails?

But remember, while clients are waiting for your reply, they are probably also shopping around. If a competitor has what they need when they need it, you may not only lose a job, but a client as well. Every enquiry could be an excellent prospect for the future, so why ignore it? If the call or email is a waste of time, just hang up or ignore it.

The better your ability to communicate quickly, effectively and positively with existing and prospective clients, the more successful you're likely to be.

7

Don't hide
your light

Translators must be invisible, say some. If a translation is good, readers should forget they're not reading the original.

True, the translator's role is to help the author of the original text find his or her voice in another language. But professional translators who lurk in the shadows don't do themselves or the profession any favours.

Unless clients know you exist and have some idea of how you work, they're likely to make poor choices the next time they need a translation. So aim for transparency in the texts you translate, but be sure to speak up before and after. Clients should know you're there, even if other readers don't.

8

Home sweet office

You may work at home barefoot and in pyjamas, but in your client's mind you need to be dressed for business and ready for work. That means having a professional email address – coolchick707@hotmail isn't quite the thing – and answering the phone professionally, not with a casual hello or a mouth full of breakfast cereal. No loud music in the background, no bickering kids, barking dogs or boiling kettles.

It also means keeping office hours. Clients expect you to be at work when they are. Where you are is less important – no need for them to know you're at your most creative curled up by the fire, cat at your feet, Bach in your earphones and an endless supply of sweet tea close at hand.

9

You can't translate
what you don't understand

Grasp the nuances of your source language, learn to read between the lines and you can draw on the rich resources of your native tongue to give full expression to the author's intent.

This freedom is only given to those with an excellent command of their source language, best acquired in the land where it's spoken. That active command also enables you to engage with clients on an equal footing, impress them with your mastery of their language, negotiate unhampered by linguistic constraints and communicate by email or phone in a natural, clear and convincing manner. The client perceives you as local, there is no threshold to cross, and you keep up to date with the latest shifts in idiom.

But be sure to keep your target language skills well honed, too. If the only paper you read is the local one, you're heading for trouble.

10

Good, you're literate!
Now get numerate

These days, the vast majority of professional translators in the western world are self-employed. The freedom can be exhilarating, and if you love wordplay and language it's easy to forget that your job extends beyond translating proper.

Don't. Because a translator in private practice is also chief financial officer, bookkeeper, marketing manager, IT director, production and QA supervisor, PR manager, cleaner and tea maker, all rolled into one.

True, some of these tasks can be outsourced. But to build a sound freelance translation business you'll need to develop skills to cover the rest. So don't lose your focus on language, but do learn to distinguish between gross and net. Do track your earnings and fine-tune your pricing. If you're not a salaried translator, the income you earn translating needs to cover your current living expenses as well as any provision for retirement.

11

Pricing – too low, too high or just right?

"How much should I charge?" ask nervous newbie translators. The answer: "It depends" – on deadline, content, style and more.

Professional associations are often forbidden by law from recommending prices, but some do conduct surveys and publish the results. You can also simply ask around, keeping in mind that translators share such information more readily with peers they've actually met.

A few rules of thumb:

- If you're swamped, your prices are too low.
- If you don't have enough work, your prices may be too high, but more likely you aren't marketing your services properly (or are a poor translator).
- If you quote a price to a prospective client and they respond "Yes!" immediately, then you're charging too little. (It's better if they wince before accepting.)

12

Nobody can be
in three places at once

It's sometimes called the iron triangle – the unbending reality that you can have something that meets two but not all three of the criteria – good, fast and cheap.

It may be possible for your clients to get a good translation quickly if they're willing to dig deep into their pockets. But if they demand a job fast and cheap, they cannot reasonably expect it to be of high quality. On the other hand, if they are prepared to wait, they may be able to get something good that is also inexpensive.

At times, it pays to remind them of this. And don't forget: people remember how well you did a job long after they've forgotten how quickly you did it.

13

Stand out
from the crowd

Urologists don't fix leaking radiators. Hairdressers don't shear sheep. Claiming proficiency in a plethora of subjects and languages usually indicates a lack of professionalism. The I-translate-everything approach also sends out signals that translation is easy, and easy tasks rarely pay well. If you want to get interesting, well-paid work, you need a unique selling point. That's why it's important to develop one or more specialist areas and stand out from the crowd.

14

Translators translate documents, not texts

Novels and essays apart, many documents include visuals, drawings and even sounds. These components are an integral part of the document and are vital to its comprehension. How can you translate a photo caption without seeing the image? How can you ensure the words match the images or the sound effects without seeing the film?

Even if as a translator you work purely on the text, you need to have the entire document in order to understand it completely and translate it effectively.

15

Blow your
own trumpet

When contacting potential clients, only give information that's relevant, not your entire CV. State your specialisms from the start to grab the reader's interest. An interest or hobby gives you specialist knowledge and terminology. So if you're crazy about gardening or golf, you can offer expertise that makes you stand out from the generalist.

Do your research. Write to a targeted individual and make sure the subjects you offer are appropriate to the kind of work involved.

And finally, check and double-check your résumé and covering note. A single spelling error or clunky construction and your letter might well end up in the bin.

16

Three skills in one – translator, writer, expert

No matter what area you specialise in, all translators need the same core skills of good subject understanding and excellent writing ability.

Take an honest look at your skillset. There are three key ingredients you need: mastery of the foreign language, the ability to write clear, incisive text in your own language and a thorough grasp of the subject matter. Most people put a lot of effort into learning the foreign language – and let's face it, that's no mean achievement. But you also need to hone your own writing skills and invest in developing them. Consider enrolling on a technical writing course, for example. Or a creative writing workshop. Then set about improving your subject knowledge and research skills.

17

Hallmarks of a good translation

Fitness for purpose, of course. And accuracy; the meaning as understood by the reader must be the same as that intended by the writer. But also faithfulness to the conventions of the target language. This usually precludes translating into a language other than your own. Why? Because the qualities that make a text sound right and flow well – register, rhythm, euphony – are often the most challenging aspects of a foreign language to master. A non-idiomatic translation is as conspicuous as a foreign accent.

Paradoxically, the footprint of a good translator should be invisible. The less noticeable your presence, the more notable your achievement.

18

Start to specialise – then dig deep

When you're just starting out, you may be tempted (or obliged) to translate everything you're offered. But that's not realistic or sustainable if you're in for the long haul and want to move beyond the bulk market.

So as you gain experience, keep an eye out for subjects that you enjoy and where there's genuine demand. Then dig in.

It's even better if you have a passion, since you'll already have at least some of the specialist knowledge you need to shine. Just be sure there's demand for it in your language combination. (Cricket? Not ideal if you work from Spanish to English.)

If you've pondered and are still drawing a blank, subscribe to a business daily for three months. Spend 20 minutes a day skimming through to identify hot topics and industries on the move. Then dig in. Deep.

19

Bilingualism is no guarantee of a good translator

Being able to write in your mother tongue does not make you a professional writer. Nor does the ability to speak two languages assure success as a translator.

Why? Because bilingualism is no guarantee that a person can successfully transfer meaning between languages and cultures. Nobody is born a translator. Accidents of birth offer no shortcuts. A professional translator's skills are the result of years of study, practice and hard work.

20

Light years apart?

"Translators are self-critical; interpreters are self-confident."

The old adage may be slightly unfair to interpreters, but it does point to a couple of essential differences.

Translators have time to mull over problems – they can (and should) revisit their translation several times to hone it. They may spend hours researching terminology, contacting the client if necessary.

Interpreters have to think on their feet. Speed and flexibility are paramount. They undertake pre-emptive research, trying to anticipate potential problems.

Not all interpreters make good translators – and vice-versa. The skills involved are different.

21

Learn from others

There's inevitably a gap between what you learn at university and the practical knowledge you need as a translator.

The best place to learn the tricks of the trade is a translation company or in-house department. If you eventually leave to set up as a freelancer, you will never regret the experience.

When you start up on your own, one way of gaining experience is to offer to proofread an established translator's work in exchange for mentoring. The best way to make useful contacts is through professional bodies, which also run workshops and training events.

22

Cultivate
your colleagues

Translation can be a lonely profession, and keeping in touch with others via telephone, email and social media makes a lot of sense. But it's even more important to get to know fellow translators face to face at conferences, seminars, professional association meetings and on professional development courses. You may find a trusted colleague willing to stand in for you while you are on holiday. Note that established translators can offer more than just support and advice – if you impress them, they may turn to you next time they need help with a project.

23

Beware
of sharks

You may find yourself receiving enquiries from unknown companies who "have found your details online". Who are they? Where are they based? Are they genuine? It's worth making discreet enquiries, or you may find you are never paid for any work you do for them. Many translator groups and professional associations have advisory lists of companies with whom members have had problems in the past.

24

The pen is mightier
than the sword

It makes sense always to send a quotation to your client and not to start the translation until you have written acceptance of your conditions. Then send an order confirmation as written proof of a mutual agreement. That helps avoid any arguments or legal proceedings later on.

A professional quotation includes a brief description of the work to be done (often specifying the number of pages or words), the delivery date(s), the cost and the terms of payment.

As regards pricing, quoting for work can be very much of a learning curve. But with each translation you complete, the process will become a little clearer and your bank balance a little healthier.

25

You only
live once

It may be all right to start your career as a translator hunched over a laptop in your favourite café, but in the long run you will have to consider creating an environment that is pleasant to work in and doesn't do long-term damage to your health.

The main strain is taken by a translator's eyes, fingers and back – so make sure you have adequate and adjustable lighting, and invest in a separate, tiltable keyboard, ergonomic seating, and a generously sized screen placed to avoid glare and reflections.

We're talking PC here, not laptop or tablet!

job.txt   job.docx   job.html

job.odt   job.pptx   job.csv

job.idml   job.mif   job.xlsx

26

Tech it
or leave it

Client needs are constantly evolving. You may be asked to localise or translate text in a huge variety of file formats, encrypt emails and attachments, work directly on a corporate server, use and update terminology in various file formats, and/or use and generate translation memories in various formats.

You don't have to accept jobs involving technologies you don't understand, but if you do accept them you should make sure you know how to use the best and latest tools efficiently.

27

Do you have a niche?

Marking yourself out from other translators is all about having a specialist area. Ideally you'll have a degree in, say, law or economics or engineering, but you can also build on a personal interest like music, art, cooking or sport. Or select an area you've already done some translation work in and expand your knowledge. The internet is a wonderful resource for this. Once you can legitimately call yourself a specialist, you can raise your prices.

28

Ask the right questions at the right time

The right time to ask questions is before you start a job or while it is in progress, not at the last minute – and certainly not when or after you deliver the finished translation.

Asking the right questions makes you look good to the client. It shows that you're on the ball, and know what you're doing. It's also an opportunity to talk, which is never a bad thing. So agree with your client on a process for handling questions; otherwise, adding queries to your finished job can make you look unprofessional – you're delivering an unfinished product.

Okay, there may be circumstances in which a translator's note is the only answer – but we can't think of any.

29

Turning junk into gems

A good translator can usually find subtle ways of turning copy produced by a less capable writer into something easier to read and more convincing than the original. That's often precisely what demanding clients want – even if they don't say so up front. It's part of the added value a skilled professional translator brings to the table.

But to be on the safe side, check with your buyer. Clarify the translation's purpose and target readership. And give a few examples, so clients can see and understand how you might make their text sing – or stick with the awkwardness, if that's what is really, truly required.

Falling back on a "garbage in, garbage out" defence is unlikely to endear you to anyone, especially if you trot it out after the event.

30

"It's not technical ... "

Many in the translation industry classify non-literary documents as either "technical" or "general", assuming that "technical" means more difficult.

If you see yourself as a generalist, be careful. Documents that clients describe as general can sometimes be very challenging. Take management-speak and human resources: the first enjoys wrapping simple ideas in woolly sentences full of buzzwords and in-house jargon, while the second frequently includes implicit references to local laws and work practices – two areas where clear-cut equivalents are rare.

Beware of accepting a text the client claims contains "nothing technical" before you have read it closely. Or you may be in for an unpleasant surprise.

31

Be a fly
on the wall

Forget cold calls and one-off pitches. Instead make a habit of hanging out where your potential clients gather. Attend their press conferences and industry events. Read their publications. Go to their trade fairs. Sign up for business get-togethers.

Talk to your targets, sure – but above all listen very carefully.

You'll learn a lot about their specialist subjects – essential knowledge once you've got a job in hand. Just as important, you'll get to know who's who, and you'll pick up the language and mindset you need to present their case effectively to their readers. This will also make it easier for you to present your own case to clients.

Good clients appreciate your passion for their subjects and their industry.

32

Clients: find the right fit for you

Build a client portfolio that's a good match for you and your skillset. Some translators enjoy the adrenalin rush of quick turnarounds, others prefer longer-term projects. Some clients seek active involvement, others simply want you to take the job off their hands.

In general, clients who are actively involved are more demanding and have larger budgets. That's not surprising: they are more aware of the benefits of getting it right and the risks of getting it wrong.

At the churn-it-out end of the spectrum, clients are less inclined to engage. That's their choice – but since it impacts on your working conditions, it's worth thinking about.

33

Invest in
yourself

Frugality can be a false economy. If you're targeting clients in the business world, do have an outfit or two that allow you to blend in with your prey (no flowing robes or flea-market specials). Discard outdated business cards rather than add a new contact address by pen. Update hardware and software regularly, and invest in continuing professional development to sharpen your skills. Join a professional association.

These are not frivolous outlays; they are smart investments in yourself and your practice. The most frugal translators are often those least visible to precisely the kinds of clients they want, or claim they want.

34

When to
say no

It's tempting to accept every job out of customer loyalty, but it's better to say no than to agree to an unrealistic deadline, or if you are ill or too busy to do a tip-top job. Clients can be fickle – one translation that isn't up to scratch and they'll take their business elsewhere. Saying you were rushed is no excuse.

Raising your price for a rush job helps focus the client's mind on how urgent it really is, while splitting large jobs with colleagues can relieve pressure.

Saying no to an assignment with a silly deadline demonstrates that you won't compromise on quality and would rather miss out on the business than turn in a sloppy job. Most clients will thank you for showing that you have their best interests at heart.

35

Add value
and sell it

Some technologies change the way people work; others change public perceptions of a profession's role and value.

Take family portrait photographers. They're disappearing fast as digital photography reduces the intrinsic value of individual photos, convincing most users they can do a "good enough" job for next to no outlay. People still recognise that professionals take better pictures; they're just reluctant to pay for the service.

Free or low-cost software can't deliver professional-quality translations. But it can transform public perceptions and is currently doing just that. To counter this, translators need to demonstrate how they add value. You're not quicker or cheaper than a computer, so prove instead that you're smarter, write better and can supply outstanding personal service. It's never crowded along the extra mile.

36

Be aware of
what's not there

Sometimes you need to translate what's not there.

In some countries letters don't start with a Dear So-and-So or end with a Yours whateverly, but if you omit such phrases in your English translation, you are doing your clients a disservice.

Some languages have no word for "please", but it's often needed in English And just as you know not always to translate the French indefinite article *des* before a plural noun, in translations from other languages you may sometimes choose to add the word "some" where the original has nothing.

37

It's your call – make friends with your phone

Source texts often contain ambiguities that you need to clarify with the client.

Do you send an email? No, pick up the phone and ask your question. If the reply is unclear, query it at once. Every dialogue is an opportunity to build a relationship, so talk to your client about the weather, her dog, your vacation plans. You become a 3D person for her; she learns you have children, cats, hay fever … And all of this in her native tongue.

Professional phone skills take years to master, particularly in a foreign language. Telesales courses help. Learn to line up your arguments and deal with criticism. And if the client calls and catches you unprepared to negotiate on a project, don't hesitate to say "Can I call you back?" Then it's your call to make when you're good and ready.

38

Join the conversation

Promotional literature drafted by in-house teams can focus on company objectives rather than client needs. Before translating them, discuss adopting a more reader-centred approach to produce a new, possibly radically different, text.

Identify the source text's assumptions concerning the target readership's familiarity with the company, its products and reputation. Discuss possible solutions with your client, then adapt accordingly. By becoming part of the conversation, you'll be seen as part of the team and the rewards will be greater.

What clients think they want and what they actually need are not necessarily the same thing. Until you ask, they may not know themselves; they surely should afterwards.

39

Good guys, bad guys

The client spectrum ranges from dismal to excellent, with many different profiles in between. (Just like translators, in fact.)

Aim for a roster of good clients, whose distinguishing features include passion, dedication and healthy budgets. Weed out less desirable candidates through strategic price hikes and unavailability.

Whatever you do, don't waste time and energy ranting about bad clients. It puts you in the wrong frame of mind and may skew your efforts to hook up with the good guys.

The best defence against cranky, underfunded, chronically hair-on-fire clients is to be so busy working with motivated, well-heeled and organised ones that you don't need them.

40

Look before
you leap

Sometimes busy clients simply email a document asking for a translation. But before you dive in, there are things you need to know.

Who is going to read it? The general public, trade press, exhibition visitors, competitors, existing clients, potential clients or potential investors? In which countries? Are there visuals? Will the layout be bilingual? Is it for a website? If going into English, is it for a UK, US or international audience? Will the translation need adapting to resonate? Might some sections be removed? Is additional information needed?

Questions like these make you look smart, not stupid. They show clients you want to understand their business and their brief.

41

Understand what the source text *doesn't* say

Unless you're truly proficient in your source language, you'll never have the confidence to make your target text sound authentic. If you don't detect the weak signals – for example that rather odd wording (Is it committee writing? Or a sign that your remarkably diplomatic authors have something to hide?) – the chances are you'll play it safe and end up with something even odder in the target language.

Living in the country where they speak your source language is the best way to stay on top of things, but that's obviously not an option for everybody. If it's been years since you set foot in the country, you need to plan a trip. Maybe even a sabbatical. Or find another way to get back into the conversation before it's too late.

42

Three paths
to direct clients

Direct clients commission translations via three channels: an in-house translation unit, Central Purchasing, or specialist functions like Corporate Communications. What are the pros and cons?

The translation unit is staffed by colleagues familiar with the challenges we face (pro) and the going rates (con).

A purchasing department sources translation like any other commodity, expects bulk buying to be cheaper and generally opts for the lowest price. Rarely familiar with our profession, they are unaware of quality issues. No pros here, just cons.

Corporate communications professionals are our soulmates – concerned with getting the message across effectively. Aware of the power of language, they appreciate attention to detail. For them, cost is often less important than quality.

43

Don't cause headaches – cure them!

Never take problems to clients. Enhance your market value by offering solutions instead. Clients already have enough headaches of their own. That's one reason why they hire you.

Identify the problem. Determine the criteria a solution needs to satisfy. Brainstorm – alone or with colleagues – as many solutions as you can. Then analyse each one to see which best matches the criteria. Now you have a solution to propose rather than a problem.

Who do you think people are happier to see: someone who gives them a headache – or someone who takes a load off their mind?

44

The worm has to taste good for the fish, not for the angler

As with any professional service, the translator must keep the client happy. That's the first rule of business.

But translation has a twist: unlike many other transactions, a translation buyer is not necessarily that translation's user. This means client needs and end-user needs may not coincide. In some cases the buyer may be unaware of the gap, or not understand the end-user's mindset and culture at all. Enter the expert translator – the person best positioned to represent the end-user, whose satisfaction is what really counts.

Satisfying the client who hires you proves you're a good salesperson. Satisfying the (absent) reader you're translating for proves you're a good translator.

45

There's more to translation than meets the eye

Translation clients should be grateful for that, because a good translator adds value. For example, when a UK firm boasts of success in "foreign markets", a translator needs to clarify that this means non-UK markets. Similarly it may be necessary to specify which country has issued "a government report" or inspired designs based on "local traditions". Likewise "the diagram below" may be "the diagram above" once a translation is typeset. "On page 12" may be "on page 13" in the final printed version.

Good translators always put themselves in their readers' shoes.

46

The more you know,
the harder it gets,
until suddenly ...

Once you begin to really understand your source language, you gradually become aware of its subtleties. That's when you start thinking about the corresponding subtleties in your target language.

If you're continually reaching for a thesaurus, you may not know exactly what it is you are looking for, but you know what you are doing – and why. You're on the right path.

On the other hand, if you are continually reaching for a bilingual dictionary to help you through a text, don't give up the day-job yet.

47

Tapping resources

Translation is about conveying ideas and emotions, preserving the logic and development of an argument. But it is also about reflecting pace, tone, flavour – idiosyncrasies, even – in order to achieve a comparable effect on the reader of the translated text.

Translation isn't about the number of words, or sentence length. A source text may use long sentences whereas it might be more appropriate for the translation to use short ones. So tap the resources of your language. Assonance, alliteration, Germanic versus Latinate vocabulary, active versus passive – these are just some of the resources available to you.

48

Two eyes good,
four eyes better

No matter how carefully you translate, no matter how accurately you type, mistakes will creep into your text. No matter how often you re-read it, you won't catch them all.

Even in a small organisation, it's usual for translators to revise each other's work; in bigger ones it's the rule.

That's not so easy when you work on your own. Revising each other's work is one of the most valuable forms of mutual support, and one of the most rewarding ways in which to build up a network of trusted colleagues.

It's not just about spotting mistakes. Revised should also mean better – your colleague may well suggest solutions you never thought of. And revisers may learn from your work things they had never thought of. It's a two-way street.

49

Professionals
vs amateurs

Professional translators earn their living translating: it's their livelihood. Most of those who make a good living (and many do) work full time; anything less and the muscles you need for the heavy mental lifting tend to atrophy.

Amateurs work for free – or near enough.

Struggling professionals usually haven't figured out where to focus their talent, or they've made bad business choices along the way. Some haven't developed the basic translation skills they need in order to succeed.

Struggling amateurs? An oxymoron. Amateurs are independently wealthy (or, possibly, independently poor) or translating for other reasons altogether.

50

Don't bury your head in the sand

You are, naturally, aware of the need to back up your work. And you may already have other kinds of back-up in place. For example, a trusted colleague to stand in for you during vacations, preferably someone who writes in a similar style. Maybe you are already revising each other's work, to your mutual benefit.

But you need to look further. Imagine you are taken ill or stranded away from home, or your office is destroyed by fire.

Don't bury your head in the sand: draw up a Plan B for various scenarios now, including business insurance, precautions before the event and emergency response after it. Discuss the issue with your colleagues; draw up joint plans. How are you going to access each other's (back-up) files? And how will the 300-page translation you have nearly finished reach the client on time?

51

Know your client

Deadlines are often set by people who think it takes you ten minutes to translate a page that took them three hours to write. They don't understand your needs. But do you understand theirs? Getting to know clients and talking to them are effective ways of making things work better for all involved.

True, an internet search tells you all you need to know about a company. But that doesn't mean you know your client. Your client is not the company, but a flesh-and-blood person who decides how the company spends its money and who gets its business. The best way to make sure that is you is to establish a good relationship with that person.

52

It may not be you

It's tempting to hazard an inspired guess when faced with an indecipherable passage – but it may not be your fault if you can't make sense of the original. Contact the client for an explanation. Perhaps the text is poorly formulated. You may not be paid to check content, but doing so adds value. The translation process often reveals poor writing, ambiguity and even factual errors. Check figures, dates and names.

Be sure to raise your queries in good time. Most clients won't think you're overstepping your brief, they'll be grateful (even impressed). And the direct contact will help cement your relationship.

53

Sometimes the original is just a pale imitation of the translation

Can a translation be better than the original? You bet! And that doesn't only apply to complex and convoluted technical texts: Nobel laureate Gabriel García Márquez famously claimed that Gregory Rabassa's English translation of *Cien años de soledad* was better than the original. Rabassa himself, comparing his task to that of the sculptors of Borobdur who revealed images of the gods "hidden" in the stone, said he simply uncovered the English concealed beneath the surface of Marquez's Spanish.

The more you chip away at your translation, the better it will be.

54

Does a rose by any other name really smell as sweet?

Some proper names need translating and it's the translator's job to find out which. For example, Hans Christian Andersen's name is known worldwide, but many languages have their own version of Copenhagen.

Most personal names, actual and fictional, present no problem. But for historical figures, the names of companies and organisations, geographical features, buildings and the titles of all sorts of creative works, it pays to do some research. Rolls Royce were certainly glad they did when they changed the name of the Silver Mist model to Silver Shadow to safeguard its appeal on the German market.

55

Mind
the gap

Different languages punctuate in different ways. Translators from French know to get rid of spaces before colons, question marks, etc. and change French guillemets to English inverted commas. The Greek question mark is a semi-colon. Routinely retaining the Scandinavian languages' exclamation marks after imperatives turns even an innocuous PTO! into a savagely barked command in English. But other punctuation marks need translating, too. Danish comma usage is so complex it has become a political concern. Punctuation can be a pain in the asterisk. You can quote us on that. Just make sure you use the right quotation marks.

56

Numbers need translating – that figures

Changing 8 p.m. to 20:00 is easy enough. But other numbers need translating, too. Whole websites are devoted to conversions of clothes sizes: UK shoe size 8 is a continental 42. US dress size 8 is 14 in the UK and 40 elsewhere in the EU. Gas mark 8 in recipes needs to be translated into Celsius or Fahrenheit to make sense outside the UK. And dates written 12/09/15 mean different things in different countries. Decimal and thousand separators need especially careful treatment: do commas need changing to points, or spaces to commas? You can probably think of tons more examples – but are they US tons, metric tonnes or imperial tons?

57

Say it
again, Sam

"Look here, Will," said Shakespeare's German translator August Schlegel, pondering the best rendering of the line, "Out, out, damned spot". "Do we really need that second 'out'?"

In many countries, it is drilled into budding writers that repetition is tantamount to admitting you were not at the front of the queue when vocabulary was handed out. But in English, repetition can be a rhetorical device, a means of building emphasis – not least in speeches, but elsewhere, too. Used wisely it will serve you well. Time after time after time.

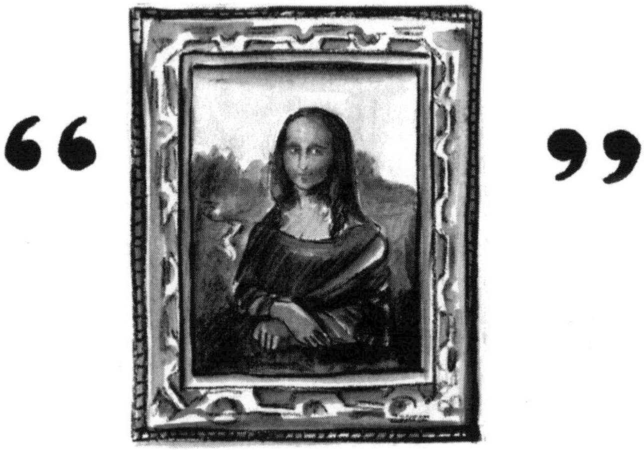

58

Notables' quotables

The rule for handling a quotation is simple: if you can find it in translation, place quotation marks around it. If you can't, paraphrase, using reported speech.

Treaties, international conventions, some national legislation and many great works of literature and music – titles and texts and libretti – can generally be found online. Google Books is just one of many invaluable resources.

Remember to acknowledge the source when citing a translation that is in copyright.

Some languages sprinkle quotation marks around phrases that are not quotations – treat with caution.

59

Judge your words
by the company they keep

While professional translators are aware of the treacherous nature of false friends, collocations present a subtler challenge. German students "hear" a lecture (*eine Vorlesung hören*), those in France "follow" it (*suivre une conférence*), whereas those in the UK "attend" it.

Sensitivity to source and target language collocations is key to achieving a natural flow in most types of translation. It is also essential for identifying novel collocations in the source language – in poetry, advertising, etc. – that require rendering with similar novelty in the target language. A collocation dictionary or a wildcard search in a web-based corpus will help you find the appropriate collocation and give your translation fluency and added impact.

60

The sound
of music

Translation is a constant tug between the twin imperatives of meaning and music.

So what is it that makes a translation sing?

It's finding the right voice – and it's precisely this nebulous notion of voice that is often overlooked because it's so hard to articulate, measure, and thus pin down.

We agonise over nuances of meaning, turn sleuth to track down a word's multiple connotations, and carefully craft sentences to ensure we've conveyed the precise sense of the source text. But there's another vital stage: making sure that the translation has rhythm, its own heartbeat, a coherent voice. Translators of poetry know this, but translators of prose also need to pay attention to music and rhythm.

61

Beware of recycling

Recycling materials is a great idea; recycling translations can be more problematical.

The idea of recycling translated blocks of text – often referred to as segments – sounds promising at first. But demanding translators know there's no such thing as a universal equivalent of even the simplest segment.

Be careful when tempted to recycle. There may be issues relating to style, register, meaning, or even all three. To be effective, a message must be tailored to the individual situation.

62

The word is
your oyster

Metaphors and idioms are a can of worms – unless you know the tricks of the trade:

- Use the same image/idiom if it exists in the target language. That's a piece of cake.
- Replace with a corresponding target language phrase. What costs an arm and a leg in English costs your shirt in Swedish.
- Replace with a simile. That often works like magic.
- Replace with an equivalent expression that rings some of the same bells as the original. "The darling buds of May" are an enigma in many countries.

63

When is a door not a door?

In all contexts, particularly technical texts, it is important to use the terms your readers themselves use. Even the simplest words that appear to convey an identical range of meaning in all languages may not be synonymous.

For instance, some languages have different words for doors between rooms and doors on cabinets, ovens, etc. A mistake here may not render a text incomprehensible, but it does signal an ignorance of the subject area. This will undermine confidence in the rest of your translation.

Subject knowledge is crucial for doing a good job, and demonstrating your expertise is a sure-fire way to impress your clients.

64

Create cross-cultural solutions

Think what teatime means to the English. The problem in conveying that in another language is equivalence. Or the lack of it. That's why English has words like intifada, chutzpah and machismo alongside rebellion, audacity and masculinity.

Words are a distillation of countless pictures, memories, allusions, connotations and contexts. In your own culture, you can assume so much. Between cultures, it is essential to make sure the full message is transferred. As a translator you need to be as fully immersed in the culture of a country as in its language, and share relevant information with the reader.

65

Rough figures
can be spot on

A translator needs to decide whether to render a figure exactly or as an approximation. The reader of a medical report wants to know the temperature of a fever as exactly in degrees Fahrenheit as in Celsius. However, an airport 20 kilometres out of town may often be described as "around 12 miles" from the city centre: precision here (12.427 miles) would be absurd.

66

Nothing gets lost in translation

More often it gets added. A lack of equivalence between the words and connotations of different languages, where each source language word contains a bit of this target-language word and a bit of that, invites the use of two words instead of one. Right or wrong? The choice is yours. As arbiter of the movement of languages across boundaries you need to look simultaneously from within and without – and decide whether anything needs to be added to preserve the sense of the original in another language.

67

Choosing the right tone

To sell the same product to diverse demographic groups, writers need to understand which voice to use. Vocabulary, idiom and register are often completely different for each group.

Translators must also be aware of current idiom, usage and register – or risk alienating the target audience. Sometimes even the street version is appropriate.

To ensure copy speaks to the reader, explore who is being spoken to. A straight translation is often not enough. There may also be cultural implications in the target market that the client is unaware of. Raise these with your client to ensure the end result is fit for purpose.

68

"We need to improve our execution!"

This message from the CEO doesn't mean she's about to call in a firing squad of management consultants. Execution = implementation. It's all part of business speak, the language that gave us *white knights* and *blue-sky thinking*. Some say business jargon is all about power, a means of excluding outsiders. For insiders, though, it's invaluable business shorthand, fostering efficient communication between specialists.

As translators, we find clients expect us to deliver business speak at the level to which they are accustomed. They're at home with *stakeholders*, rather than *interest groups*, aim for *benchmarks* and aspire to *raise the bar*. But don't go mining business media for every single one of the latest buzzwords; if used to excess they are likely to overtax your audience. We need to master business speak and judiciously spice our prose with it – improving our own execution.

69

Coming to terms

The need for consistent terminology varies with language, subject matter and genre. Some situations call for rigorous consistency, others for imagination and creativity. Assess your client's needs. Is repetition a virtue or a vice in this specific case? What suits a technical manual is unlikely to suit a magazine article. Get the balance right.

When choosing a terminology management tool, consider the kind of texts you usually handle. Make sure any quality assurance process or program you use meets the terminological needs you've identified.

Remember, too, that terminology can differ from company to company. Check whether your client has a standard way of translating certain specialist terms. Is there an in-house glossary? If not, you may be able to develop one as a paid add-on.

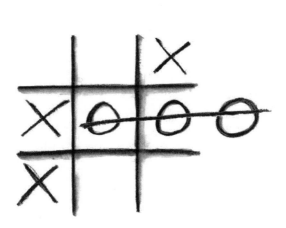

70

Think outside the box

"Can you speak?" William Brown asks a reticent Violet Bott in one of Richmal Crompton's *Just William* books.

"Yeth," lisps Violet.

Most languages have a verb for "to lisp". But to translate Violet's reply into Swedish as "Ja, läspade Violet" (as in an early translation of *William in Trouble*) suggests a dexterity of tongue that few possess. Faithfully translating the original is never enough if the result makes no sense to your target language reader. Even when faced with the most prosaic texts, you need to keep your wits about you and come up with creative solutions.

71

Your word is my command

Judicious use of inverted commas can often solve the problems caused by essential literal renderings and neologisms in translated texts. They provide a convenient way of remaining faithful to the original without taking full responsibility for a word or turn of phrase that may be unfamiliar or seem inelegant to the reader – as, for example, in IKEA's declared ambition to serve the interests of "the many people".

72

Beware of dictionaries

Dictionaries are great tools but rarely solve translation problems completely. That's hardly surprising, given that ideas can be expressed in many different ways depending on the context. If you think you have found the right word in a dictionary, always check it online and see whether/how it is used in the subject area you are working in. Never just say to yourself: "It was in the dictionary, so it must be right."

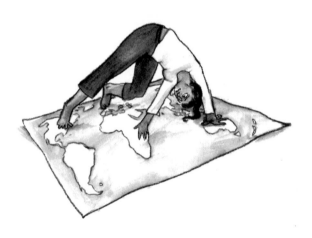

73

You can't fool all of the people all of the time

Writing mid-Atlantic English is usually no more successful than attempting to land on the mid-Atlantic ridge. And the same applies to other major languages with their regional variants.

It's not just a matter of spelling or vocabulary. There are so many differences in punctuation, capitalisation, prepositions and turns of phrase that you are bound to be found out – and a miss is often as good as a mile.

You pride yourself on being a specialist in a particular language combination and subject matter? Then take the principle a bit further: stay within your comfort zone and specialise in the language variant that comes naturally to you. And educate your clients: make them aware that a one-size-fits-all solution is unlikely to be a good fit for anything at all.

74

Revision: park overnight and use your ears

Even with a tight deadline, try to set your translation aside overnight and revise the next day with fresh eyes and a clear mind. Otherwise read it in bite-sized chunks with a few minutes' break between each one. If there really is no time, simply changing the font or character size of your text before revising can carve out some useful mental distance between draft and review. Many professionals swear by revising on paper rather than on screen.

Read your draft out loud. Often your ear will identify hitches, glitches and sections that need more work for optimum flow. And don't forget details like headlines, page numbers and captions.

75

Mind your language!

Many would-be translators focus on their foreign language skills and forget that the quality of their translation ultimately depends on their ability to express themselves in the language they are translating into. That's a big mistake.

As a translator, you are a writer. And your writing skills must be better than 98 per cent of the general population (including university graduates).

But it doesn't stop there. After all, language evolves. Don't rest on your laurels. Track developments and usage – not to embrace passing fads willy-nilly, but to incorporate developments that will make your texts more effective in an ever-changing environment.

76

IT has limits – you have none

Translation is a craft involving hard-won skills, flair and creativity; machine translation is engineering. Your work involves being a faithful, yet excitingly creative renderer of other people's ideas and feelings. Computers don't deal with ideas or feelings, only with zeroes and ones. You may be able to translate compelling marketing copy, but have you ever tried running a slogan or advertising pitch through translation software?

That said, don't go rubbishing the work of MT developers – some of your clients may be impressed by their brilliance. As a professional, you need to stay up to speed with the latest language technology, but keep honing your writing skills. They will take you where no translation software ever can.

77

Plausibility
dulls the mind

Post-editing a bad machine translation involves simple decisions: you either battle to make it better or advise that the text be retranslated from scratch.

The big challenge is reviewing a "good" machine translation. Everything looks right, but is it? Has the software read between the lines? Did it pick up the risqué innuendo? Has it remembered what was written three paragraphs before? Does the text flow? Is it compelling?

Watch out for the speciously well-formed sentence. There's nothing like plausibility to dull the mind.

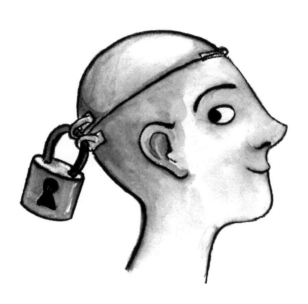

78

Mum's
the word

Can you keep a secret? Treat all the information you are asked to translate as confidential. In many cases this duty of confidentiality is written into your professional association's code of conduct.

If you consider accepting a job you can't handle alone, always request the client's approval before working with someone else. Then ask your colleague to sign a non-disclosure agreement and keep it on file.

You can also use confidentiality as a selling point with direct clients. Translation agencies cannot guarantee their suppliers do not sub-contract or work in public spaces. But you can – so don't be afraid to shout it out.

79

Talk the talk, walk the walk

"If it swims like a duck and quacks like a duck, then it probably is a duck."
But it might just also be the work of an extremely competent translator.

Translating words accurately is just the start: you also need to convince
your readers that they're looking at a piece of original writing. So you need
to quack and swim – sorry, talk and walk – the way they do, whether they're
journalists or nuclear physicists. Your writing (note: writing not translation)
will improve immeasurably. There's pleasure to be had from turning an
elegant phrase; and the icing on the cake is that research shows linguistic
puzzling may even help prevent memory loss. Quack.

80

It's not all over until the fat lady sings

Is formal translator training with its many unidentified texts and excerpts to blame? Professional translators should always make sure they translate everything in the source text.

In a magazine article, for instance, that includes straplines, captions, footnotes and full details of the source and date of publication. For corporate brochures and catalogues it may include headers, footers and possibly even an ISSN reference. It's not a fat lot of good delivering a job before it's fully completed.

81

Squeezing information into so little space is a big challenge for subtitl

Ever tried fitting a ten-letter answer into six squares in a crossword grid? Then you'll understand that subtitlers need to work magic. Every few seconds they turn dozens of words of dialogue into just a few characters in two succinct lines of text. It's hard work, of course, and far more time-consuming than standard translation: capturing the essence of what is said with all its idiomatic and cultural nuances in coherent, semantically self-contained texts that are left on screen for just the right length of time.

Subtitling is not for the faint-hearted – nor for fearless dilettantes. If you are interested in it, contact your professional association to ask for advice. Maybe you'll find a mentor willing to share the secrets of their wizardry.

82

Boomerangs

You may receive requests for translation "for information only" – the implication being that your text is only going to be used in-house and you therefore don't need to produce a polished translation. But you have no control over what happens to your rough translation further down the line. It may end up being circulated more widely, or even published. To ensure that it doesn't come back to haunt you, specify that the translation is "for information only" in a footer or watermark and include a disclaimer in your covering email.

83

All present
and correct

You are not translating for yourself, but for the client who pays you and for the reader who needs to understand you. Also, in many instances, for the communicator, web designer or typesetter who is the intermediary between you and your audience.

Make sure your translation is clearly structured. Mark it if necessary, so that even someone with no knowledge of the target language can easily see exactly what in your translation corresponds to what in the original.

Often the quality of the presentation is the only aspect of a translation a client is able to judge.

84

Hands on
the wheel

The electronic safety systems in your car can take the strain out of driving, but you still need to stay alert and keep your hands on the wheel. Similarly, there are many useful technology tools available to translators – from online dictionaries to translation memory and speech recognition – all of which promise to enhance productivity. Don't forget, though, that the corollary of faster production of the raw translation is usually more time spent on preparing and polishing the final version. So don't be tempted to rely too much on the machine.

85

Don't get caught
by the internet

It's a great feeling to find an English equivalent for a foreign-language term on the internet. And in the right context, too. But be careful to check the URL. If the web address is not in an English-speaking country, you're probably dealing with someone else's attempt at a translation – and it might not be right. Use every source of information you can find. But don't trust any of them!

86

Google Translate™
doesn't

Google Translate™ takes seriously an entreaty ascribed to Wittgenstein, "Don't ask for the meaning, ask for the use".

Trawling vast archives of translated material – media reports, UN treaties, children's novels, corporate propaganda, etc. – Google Translate™ uses probability to compute the likeliest meaning based on context.

Sometimes it works, but in a different way from translation. Just as a helicopter and a hummingbird work in different ways to hover in the air. A chopper may be fine in an emergency, but it would be in a spin to outdo a hummingbird in terms of precision and elegance.

87

Google remembers everything

Machine translation is getting better all the time; for example, Google deploys vast server farms to deliver multiple pages of translation in seconds. But Google stores and indexes everything it comes across while crawling the web. And it will store your source text and the translation Google Translate™ produces.

Tempted to use it to create a first draft and save yourself some typing and thinking? Think again: if you put your text into Google without your client's consent, you could be breaching copyright and confidentiality obligations.

88

The customer is always right. Or is she?

Sexism in language takes many different forms. In English, doctors, judges, teachers, translators, etc. tend to be referred to as "he" and nurses or carers are automatically called "she". You can sometimes get round this by using "they".

Where the noun itself traditionally reveals the person's gender, you can use a neutral version in some cases – changing "chairman" to "chairperson" or even just "chair". Times change: "actress" has now been largely replaced by "actor" and "poetess" by "poet".

The issue may not arise in the original text, where it's the word itself that's gendered. But it's something translators need to think about and develop strategies for dealing with elegantly.

89

Keep your
edge with CPD

See pee what? CPD – continuing professional development – helps you stay on top of your game and gives you a commercial edge. Some professional bodies actually require it. But it needn't mean being lectured at in dusty seminar rooms. CPD can be formal (workshops, webinars, distance learning), semi-formal (getting to grips with a CAT tool, visiting a trade fair in your field), or informal (reading the press or gleaning tips from fellow professionals over coffee at events).

If you sometimes find freelancing lonely, CPD can be socially beneficial, too. And if all that hasn't convinced you, you may even be able to offset the cost against tax as well.

90

Look at the page – and yourself

Those finely crafted words on the page (or on screen) are your final destination. But the journey there is up to you and it reflects where you position yourself in the market.

For example, you can start with careful reading, research, identification of your author's target audience and voice, and analysis of the explicit and implicit messages you need to relay. Draft. Move on to direct interaction with your client or author to tease out every nuance. And then rework, rethink, polish.

Or you can blast through, shoot your text out into a black hole in space, and jump into the next job.

You'll find clients for both approaches. How you work shapes the text on your page, but also determines what you can charge and your job satisfaction or burnout.

91

Lock up
your words

Your words are precious – often literally so. An expert can unlock an industrial secret from a single sentence. And if you translate financial, legal, scientific or technical documents, your translations will certainly be of interest to somebody out there.

Ask your clients about the level of security they expect from you. Better still, take the lead on security: install an anti-spyware program, use strong passwords, make encrypted e-mail attachments the norm, don't ask untrusted experts for terminology advice or discuss clients' work in the social media, never turn off your firewall and don't work in public places with your Wi-Fi on. If you upload a document or translation memory to the Cloud without the express consent of your client, you may be putting their assets and your own at risk.

Pride yourself on being known as the "cautious translator".

92

Explain yourself

To clients who don't know your language, your translation is as unintelligible as a Jackson Pollock painting. Others compare it word for word with the original.

If you have reorganised the text in any way, added a clarification (explaining a cultural reference or geographical location) or removed something irrelevant to the reader (information that only applies to the country of origin), you can forestall client queries by appending a few words in a covering email or email attachment to explain and justify your actions.

93

The quality of mercy
is not strained

A good translation satisfies the client, is fit for purpose and true to the original. However, client approval and fitness for purpose signal success rather than quality, while accuracy is no guarantee of elegance.

Any translation – yours, too – is open to censure.

So be sparing in your criticism of the work of professional colleagues, especially if you are unfamiliar with the brief they were given. And if anyone does criticise your work, try to learn from their comments.

94

Take responsibility and get credit

Lots of clients won't be able to judge the translation you deliver – after all, it's in another language. The same applies to many typesetters and designers, which makes life particularly tricky when there are last-minute changes.

To avoid stumbling at the finish line, you need to stay involved throughout the revision, layout and proof stages.

Factor this into your quotes and be prepared to go the extra mile. In exchange, explain to clients that your name goes in the credits as translator. It costs them nothing, gives you an added incentive to produce fine work, and allows new clients to track you down.

95

Don't pile it – file it

Record-keeping is boring, and most of us will find excuses to avoid it. But staying on top of it reduces stress and frees up time for the more creative aspects of translation.

How you keep your records is entirely up to you, but be systematic. Ideally update them after every job or payment, and at least once a week. Little and often really is less painful than infrequent but long sessions with piles of invoices or receipts. Knowing what's due when will help you to keep on top of payments and improve your cash flow. And you'll have your ammunition ready when clients "haven't received the invoice", express wonder that payment is overdue, or claim they didn't know what you charge.

96

Be
transparent

Successful translators often have to outsource work to colleagues when they have no capacity themselves. If you do so, it's best to inform your client. And remember, you must take complete responsibility for the quality of the final text, checking it carefully and editing it as necessary before sending it off. It's never a good idea to pass off someone else's work as your own.

97

Professional ethics: clients

Most of the precepts behind professional ethics apply to everyday life: only occasionally does something arise which relates specifically to your job as a translator.

For client relations you must build trust by:

- Being honest about your qualifications, capabilities and responsibilities, and working within them.
- Negotiating agreed terms of business, and abiding by them. Most professional organisations offer model terms and conditions that can serve as a basis for your own.
- Keeping confidential information confidential.

98

Professional ethics: colleagues

Be professional in your dealings with colleagues:
- Be willing to share knowledge and experience.
- Negotiate and abide by agreed terms of business (yes, it applies to colleagues, too).
- As a first recourse, endeavour to resolve professional disputes through a professional body.

Most professional associations have a code of conduct or ethics; they should also have an ethics committee to enforce it. Find out about your own association's code and its mediation and/or arbitration procedures.

99

Keep calm –
and keep the client

No matter how brilliant you are, at some point a client will complain about your work. How you react will determine your future with that client.

So don't explode, but don't grovel either. Express concern that there's a problem and ask for specific examples. Examine these in detail.

If you failed to supply enough information to back up your translation choices, do so now (in the client's own language). If improvements are needed, make them. If a less-than-fluent client has second-guessed you on vocabulary and style, don't despair or spin out of control. Win them over by offering a third option instead.

Making a confident case for your work while indicating that you're flexible enough to incorporate suggestions is a sign of professionalism.

100

You hold the copyright, right?

Let's face it. Sometimes things go from bad to worse.

If a client is unwilling to pay, a reminder that you hold the copyright in the translation until payment is received may resolve the situation and save you having to resort to lengthy legal or arbitration procedures.

101

Rules are made
to be broken

There are no hard and fast rules in translation, just as there are none for speaking or writing. There are conventions, recommendations and accepted forms for how to communicate, but ultimately it's up to you how you use these. In *Politics and the English Language*, George Orwell lays down five points for good writing. Then he adds a sixth: "Break any of these rules sooner than say anything outright barbarous."

The same applies to the advice in this book. Ponder the problems. Choose what you feel comfortable with. Reject what does not work. You are the translator. You and your client must be satisfied with the result you produce. It is your work, your reputation and your livelihood.

The people
behind 101 Things

WLF Think Tank is an ad hoc organisation, a virtual body of experienced practising translators that has met as the WordLink Forum at frequent intervals since 1995 to discuss the state of the profession. Its members include keynote speakers at translation conferences, teachers of translation, and prominent exponents of the profession on three continents. Among those who have contributed content to *101 Things a Translator Needs to Know* are the following:

Paul Boothroyd (MA, Oxon; MITI) read modern languages at Oxford, trained in service industry marketing, and from 1984–1991 was Head of Language Services with translators' cooperative InTra eG in Stuttgart. In 1991, together with his wife Monika (Dipl. Übers.), Paul founded Bauer-Boothroyd Übersetzungen, a niche operation based in Schorndorf, southwest Germany. BBÜ works for blue-chip clients in German-speaking countries, translating between English and German and specialising in automotive, management, marketing, HR and sustainability material.

Carmelo Cancio is a French-to-Spanish and English-to-Spanish translator and consultant based in south-west France. In 1990 he founded Cancio Communications, specialising in creative translation with a focus on new technologies and corporate communications. Carmelo holds a Ph.D. in Spanish and a master's in English philology, and currently teaches translation at Université de Toulouse-II. He is an active member and former vice-president of SFT, a founding member of Asetrad (Spain), a sworn translator with the Cour d'Appel in Agen, the author of *La traduction professionnelle en France*, and a regular presenter of workshops for professional translators.

Chris Durban has translated financial and business texts from French to English for demanding corporate clients for over 35 years. An active member of ATA, ITI and SFT, she was president of SFT for several years, and was awarded ATA's Gode Medal in 2001. Chris has written client-education materials including *Translation, Getting it Right*, now available in 15 languages, and *The Prosperous Translator*, a compilation of business advice for translators. Co-organiser of SFT's summer school for financial translators and "Translate in the Catskills", she was an adviser to the EU's Optimale programme, and is a frequent speaker at workshops and conferences.

Steve Dyson (BSc, Physics & Maths, Melbourne) is a French-to-English translator specialising in technical journalism (steve-dyson.blogspot.com). An early innovator, he has long promoted applied best practice in English-language technical writing and communication to promote the products, services and corporate image of French industrial clients. He has compiled and published glossaries on satellite-based remote sensing and naval defence. Steve is based in Lisbon, Portugal, and in south-west France.

Andy Evans studied modern languages at Westfield College London and the Sorbonne. In 1980 he joined the European Commission's Luxembourg translation service, where for 25 years he specialised increasingly in economics, financial, statistical and, ultimately, high-level political translation. In 2003 he was appointed *Chevalier de l'Ordre de Mérite civil et militaire d'Adolphe de Nassau*. He was a founder member of ITI and currently chairs its Professional Conduct Committee. From 2005 to 2014 he represented ITI on the Council of FIT. Before all that he was a taxman.

Janet Fraser has a first degree in translation and interpreting, an MA in Sociolinguistics and another in Modern German Studies. She began her career as an in-house translator and then worked as a multilingual journalist before moving into an academic post training translators. Since 2010 she has been freelancing as a translator, examiner and editor. Janet is also actively involved in the professional scene and regularly gives talks, workshops and webinars. A lifelong linguist, her proudest language-learning experience was mastering ancient Egyptian hieroglyphs for a Diploma in Egyptology.

Catherine Anne Hiley was born to English and Canadian parents, grew up in Germany and studied in London, Berlin and Vancouver, graduating with a diploma in Fine Arts from the Kunsthochschule Berlin-Weissensee in 2007. In 2008 she moved to Scotland where she became a member of Edinburgh Printmakers. Catherine is currently based in Edinburgh, where she works as a freelance illustrator and printmaker. She maintains a website at www.cahiley.com

Ian Hinchliffe worked as a butcher, greengrocer, bus conductor, accounts clerk and merchant navy purser before discovering the allure of translation. A former Head of Corporate Language at IKEA he was copywriter for IKEA's UK catalogue from 1989 to 1999. Ian has a Ph.D. in Scandinavian Languages and has taught Swedish, Norwegian and Translation Studies at universities and schools in the UK, Norway and Sweden. In 2004 he received the Erik Wellander Prize from the Swedish Language Council for his co-authorship of *Swedish: A Comprehensive Grammar*. He is a founder member of SFÖ.

Inga-Beth Hinchliffe (BA Hons, German & Swedish, UK; Cand. Mag., English, Norway) is a translator and owner of the translation company AB Språkman in Sweden. Inga-Beth has worked with languages and translation for her entire adult life, as a foreign correspondent, copy editor, teacher and translator of marketing texts, children's books and works on theology and biblical history. She was Executive Secretary of SFÖ from its inception in 1991 to 1998 and has been a long-standing member of SFÖ's Professional Standards Committee. Inga-Beth has also written two popular vegetarian cookbooks.

Hugh Keith studied modern languages at Oxford and trained as a teacher at York University. After teaching at a German university and a school in London he joined Heriot-Watt University, Edinburgh, where he discovered the world of translation and interpreting. In 1992 Hugh hit mid-life crisis, broke free and became a freelance translator working for the German market and running English workshops for professional translators and interpreters (www.xchange-services.co.uk/workshops). He has been external examiner at a number of UK universities and served on the ITI Conference Committee and as Convenor of the ITI Scottish Group.

Terence Lewis, MITI, entered the world of translation as a brother in an Italian religious order, entrusted with translating the founder's speeches into English. His religious studies also called for a knowledge of Latin, Greek and Hebrew. After some years in South Africa and Brazil, Terence returned to the UK and worked as a lexicographer, playwright and translator of texts as diverse as Mongolian cultural legislation (for Unesco) and a book by a minor French existentialist. He also wrote a Dutch–English machine translation application since used to translate documentation for some of the largest engineering projects in Dutch history. For the past 15 years he has devoted himself to the study and development of translation technology.

Bill Maslen studied French and German at Oxford and Tübingen, then made abortive attempts to become a sculptor and opera singer before embarking on a career as a conference interpreter. Exhausted by the stress, he worked as a senior manager for two international translation companies before setting up The Word Gym in 1990 – a language consultancy specialising exclusively in transcreation and multilingual copywriting for major corporate clients and marcomms agencies across Europe. Bill himself writes and translates for French and German clients, advises them on linguistic issues, and enjoys speaking at conferences. He is currently building a team to develop the ultimate computer-assisted translation and authoring system.

Terry Oliver, MITI, has a joint BA in German and Geology from Keele University. In 1971 he joined Unilever Germany as a staff translator, later becoming head of department. Since 1984 he has worked as a freelance technical translator (German–English), covering a wide range of content with an increasing focus on the law and technology of environmental issues. A member of BDÜ since 1980 and ADÜ Nord since 1997, he served as chairman of the latter from 2001 to 2005. He was a member of the German committee for European Standard EN 15038 and of the ISO working group on translating and interpreting. Elected to the Steering Committee of FIT Europe in 2002, he was its secretary from 2005 to 2008.

Nick Rosenthal, MITI, has worked as a technical translator from French and German since 1986. He studied languages at Salford University, and then worked as a management accountant for a large multinational company before founding SalfTrans, a specialist translation and localisation company, in 1988. Nick has a broad vision of the translation industry, with a particular interest in training and professional development. Nick chaired the Board of the ITI from 2011 to 2013.

Ros Schwartz, FITI, is an award-winning literary translator and a prominent figure in the Translators' Association of the Society of Authors. A freelancer since 1980, Ros has translated some 60 works of fiction and non-fiction, particularly novels by contemporary francophone writers. She runs numerous workshops, is a frequent speaker on the international circuit and publishes articles on translation-related issues. Ros was Chair of CEATL from 2000–2009 and is Chair of English PEN's Writers in Translation programme. In 2009 she was made *Chevalier de l'Ordre des Arts et des Lettres*.

Rannheid Sharma (MCIL, DipTransIoLET, MEI) is an English-to-Norwegian technical, pharmaceutical and medical translator. Having initially worked in other fields, she was smitten by the computer bug and started working as a software/hardware localiser, before going fully freelance in 1986. She is an experienced teacher and examiner of Norwegian at all levels and has also taught translation studies. Rannheid has been actively involved in the work of the Chartered Institute of Linguists. She chairs the London Society and used to write its newsletter. She is a board member of the Institute's Educational Trust and is passionate about mentoring.

John Smellie (BA Hons, Bradford University) worked in-house for an industrial equipment manufacturer in Paris before going freelance in 1984 and later running a successful translation business with offices in Paris and Toulouse. He moved to California in 1997 and currently owns and operates E-Files, Inc., an independent group of translators, editors and business writers providing local content and marketing communication support to the aerospace, defence and high-tech industries worldwide.

Lois Thomas started working life as an accountant but soon discovered this was not for her. She gained a degree in Occupational Psychology specialising in work group dynamics and qualified with the CIPD in Human Resource and Industrial Relations Management. Having headed up the HR function in a diverse range of businesses – from government to international manufacturing and professional organisations such as the Royal College of Physicians – she joined Bill Maslen at The Word Gym as Operations Director in 1992. Her background in work group dynamics has served her well in multilingual project management and in her external consultancy/training work for the ITI.

WLF Think Tank would also like to thank its other members for their valuable insights and input over the years, especially Cate Avery, Graham Cross, Niki Watts and Tom West.

In addition, the authors gratefully acknowledge the debt they owe to numerous experienced and insightful colleagues in the worldwide translation community who, through their books, blogs and conference presentations, have shared and inspired many of the ideas now collected in *101 Things a Translator Needs to Know*.

Professional associations mentioned above

ADÜ Nord Assoziierte Dolmetscher und Übersetzer in Norddeutschland e.V. (Association of Interpreters and Translators in Northern Germany): *www.adue-nord.de*

ATA American Translators Association: *www.atanet.org*

BDÜ Bundesverband der Dolmetscher und Übersetzer e.V. (Federal Association of Interpreters and Translators): *www.bdue.de*

CEATL European Council of Literary Translators Associations: *www.ceatl.eu*

CIoL Chartered Institute of Linguists: *www.iol.org.uk*

FIT Fédération Internationale des Traducteurs/International Federation of Translators: *www.fit-ift.org*

ITI Institute of Translation and Interpreting: *www.iti.org.uk*

PEN English PEN: *www.englishpen.org/translation*

SFÖ Sveriges Facköversättarförening (Swedish Association of Professional Translators): *www.sfoe.se*

SFT Société française des traducteurs (French Translators Association): *www.sft.fr*

TA Translators Association of the Society of Authors: *www.societyofauthors.org/translators-association*

Index of topics